The Fauré Élégie Study Book

for Cello

by Cassia Harvey

CHP319

©2017 by C. Harvey Publications All Rights Reserved.

www.charveypublications.com

The Fauré Élégie Study Book for Cello   1

Note: The Élégie is broken up into sections in this study book. The complete Élégie is at the back of the book.

Élégie
Part One: Measures 1-9

Élégie, Op. 24 by Gabriel Fauré
Exercises by Cassia Harvey

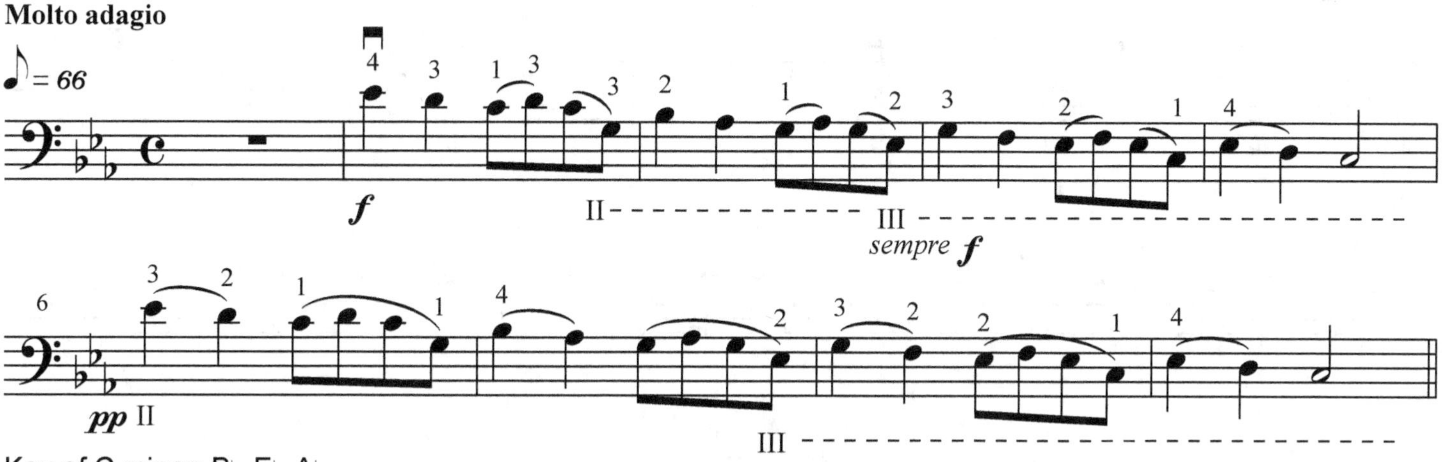

Key of C minor: B♭, E♭, A♭

Note: I = A string   II = D string
III = G string   IV = C string

Learning the Positions
Measures 2-5

©2017 C. Harvey Publications All Rights Reserved.

The Fauré Élégie Study Book for Cello

Learning the Positions
Measures 6-9

Double Stops for Intonation: Measures 6-9

String Crossing: Measures 2-9

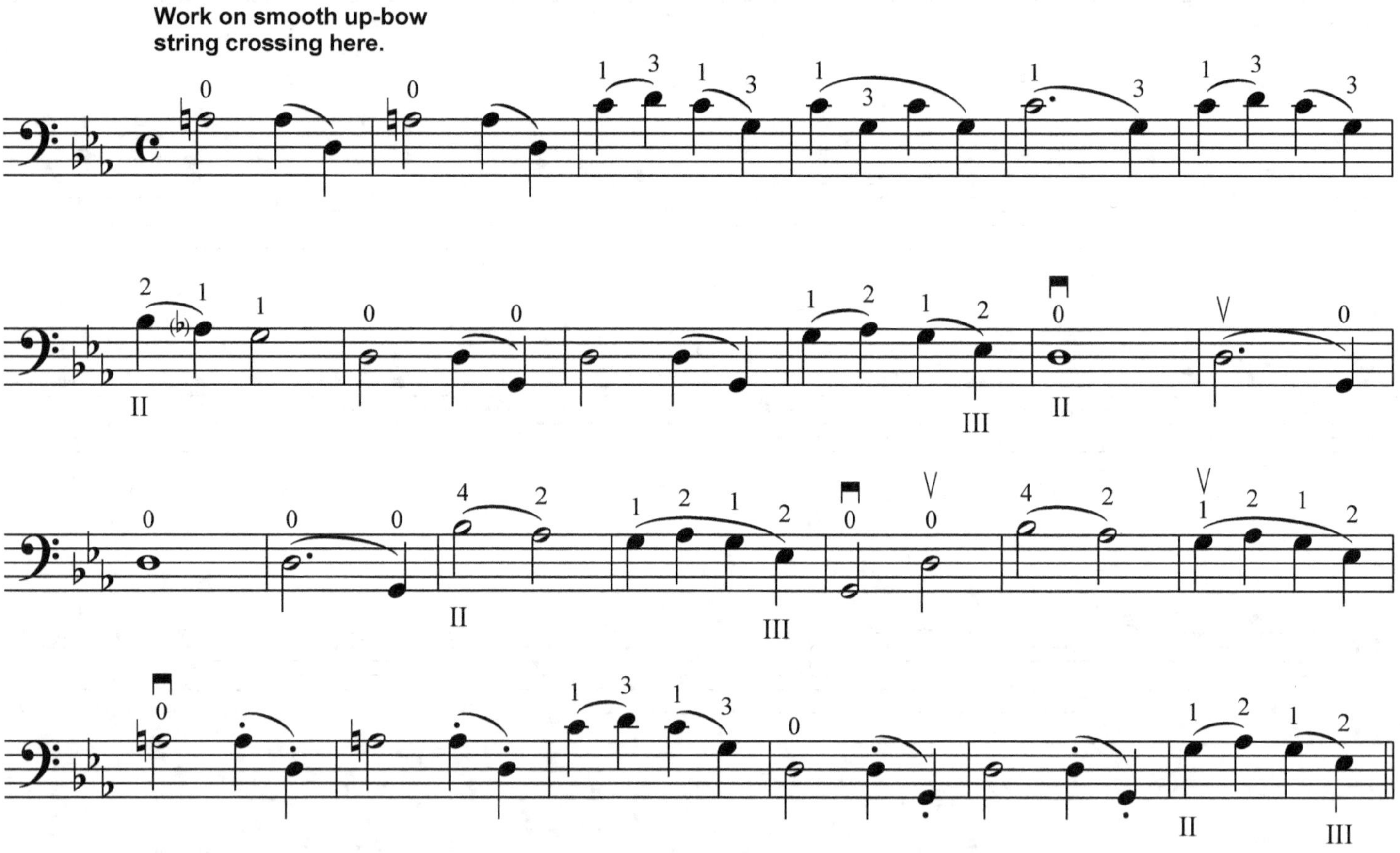

Work on smooth up-bow string crossing here.

Backward Shifting: Measures 5-9

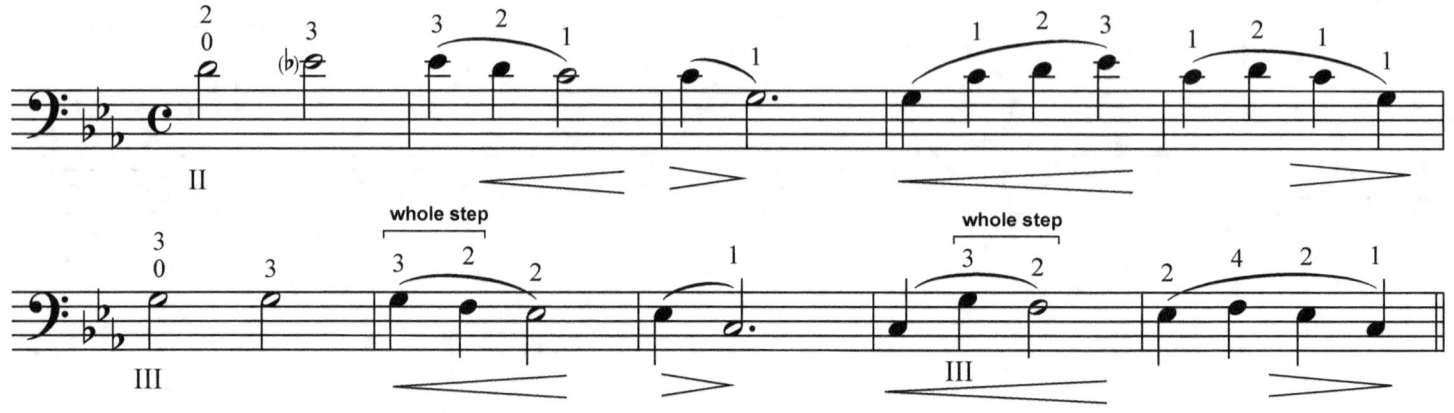

Return to play the excerpt on p.1 before continuing with p.5.

The Fauré Élégie Study Book for Cello

Élégie
Part Two: Measures 10-17: Fingering #1

(Molto adagio)

♪ = 66

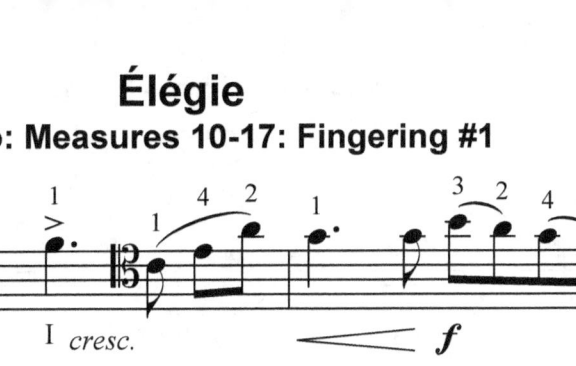

Learning the Notes: Measures 10-13

Moderato

♩ = 66 - 80

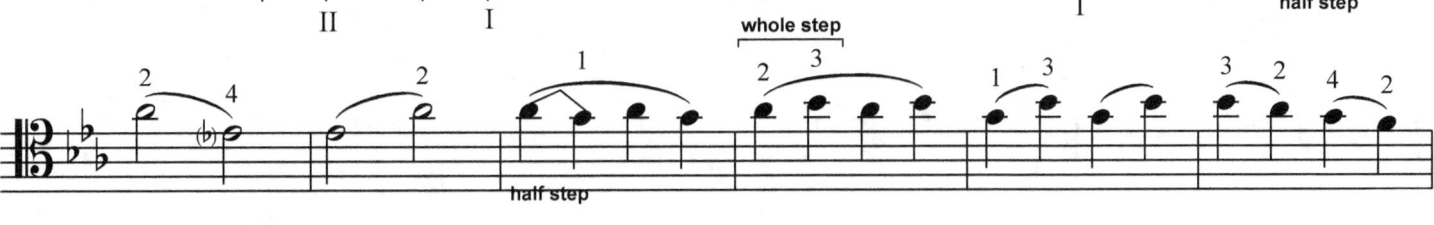

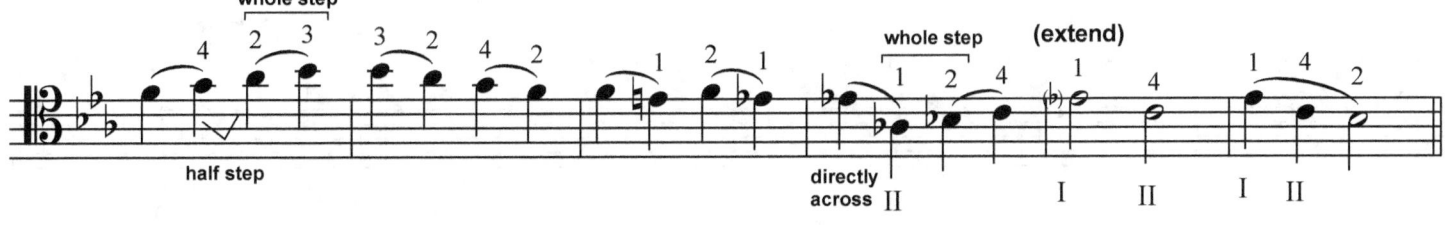

©2017 C. Harvey Publications All Rights Reserved.

Playing the Positions
Measures 10-13

Learning the Notes
Measures 14-17

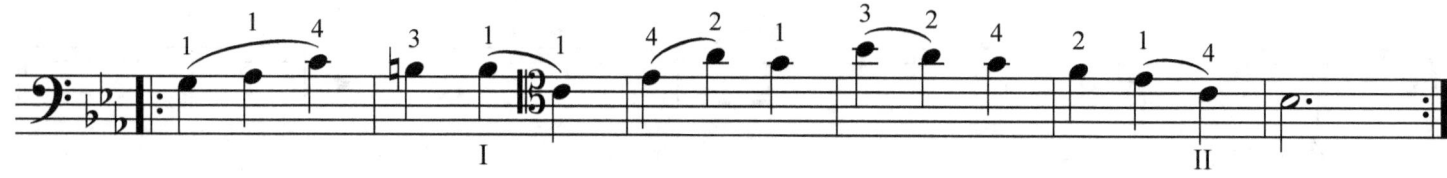

The Fauré Élégie Study Book for Cello

Shifting Study
Measures 10-17

Finger Exercise: Measures 10-17

Counting: Measures 10-17

♪ = 66
staccato; on string

Return to play the excerpt on p.5 before continuing with p.8.

©2017 C. Harvey Publications All Rights Reserved.

Élégie
Part Three: Measures 17-29

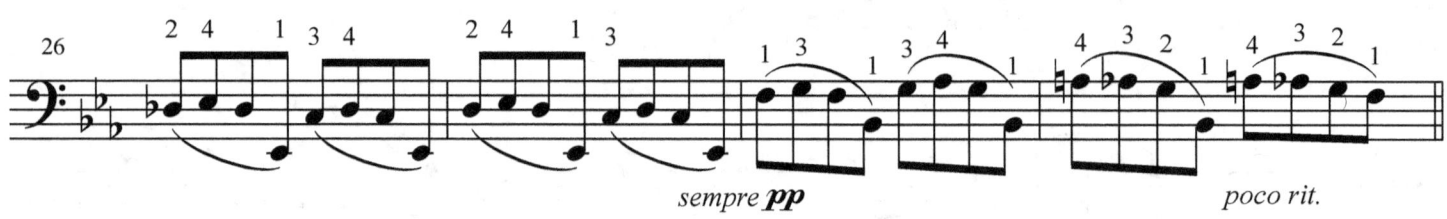

Learning the Notes
Measures 17-22

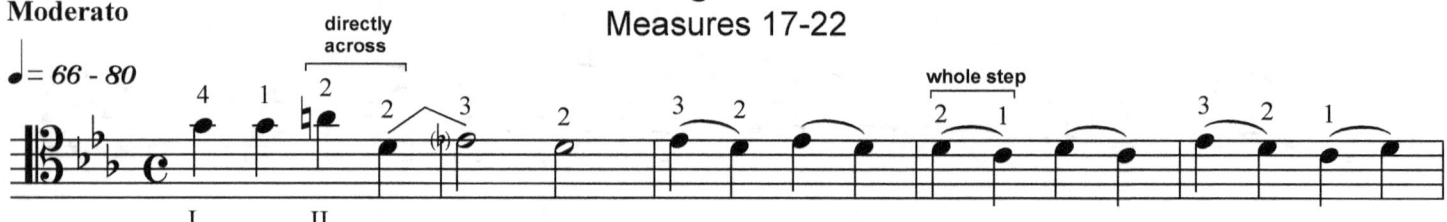

©2017 C. Harvey Publications All Rights Reserved.

Learning the Notes
Measures 24-26

Shifting
Measures 26-27

Learning the Notes
Measures 28-29

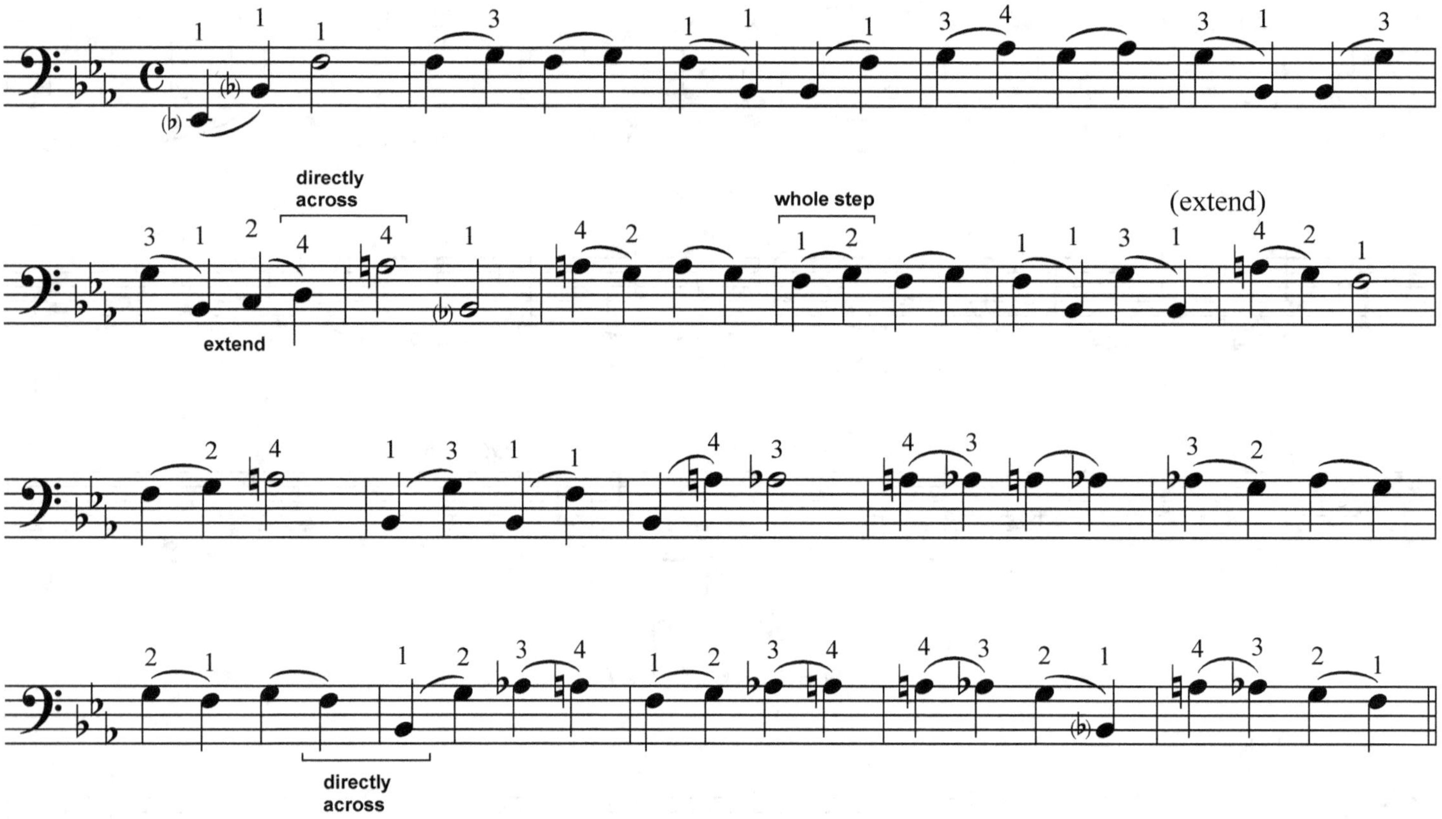

Double Stops for Intonation
Measures 23-29

The Fauré Élégie Study Book for Cello

String Crossing
Measures 23-29

Bow Control I
Measures 23-29

©2017 C. Harvey Publications All Rights Reserved.

Bow Control II
Measures 23-29

String Crossing II
Measures 23-29

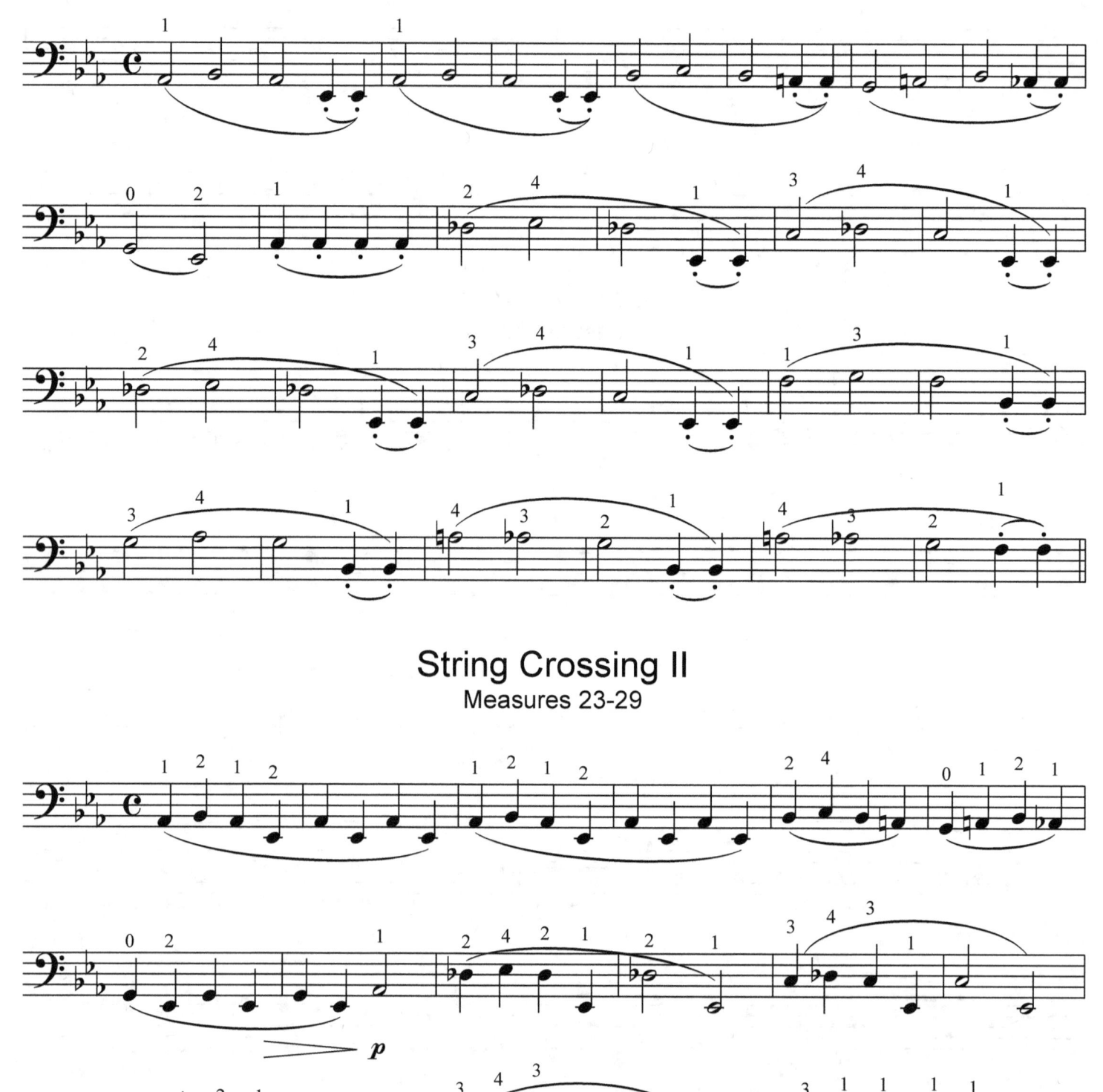

Return to play the excerpt on p.8 before continuing with p.13.

Learning the Rhythm with Half and Quarter Notes
Measures 30-31

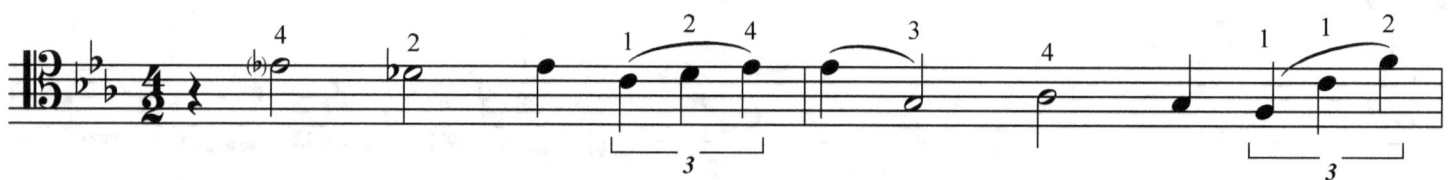

Learning the Rhythm with Quarter and Eighth Notes
Measures 30-31

Learning the Notes and Shifts
Measures 30-31

©2017 C. Harvey Publications All Rights Reserved.

Double Stops for Intonation
Measures 30-31

Shifting Backwards Across Strings: Measure 32a

Learning the Notes: Measure 32a

Two Notes in a Bow
Measure 32a

Three Notes in a Bow
Measure 32a

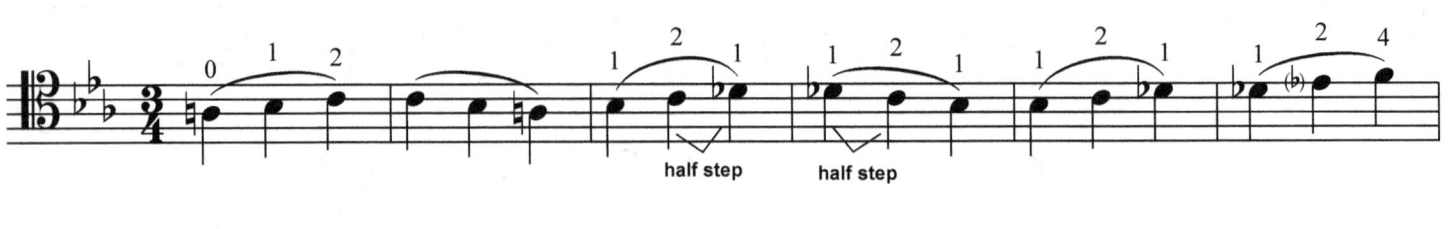

Four Notes in a Bow
Measure 32a

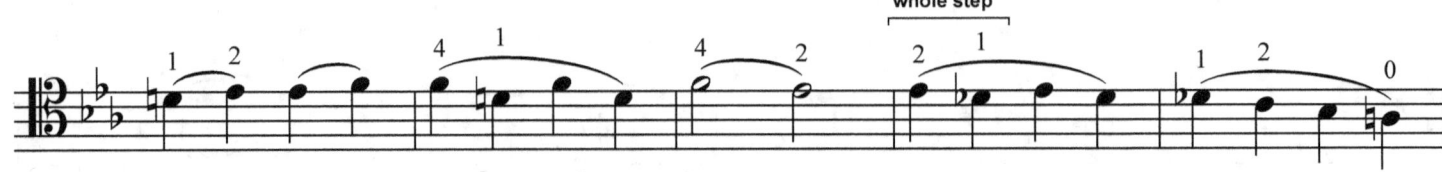

©2017 C. Harvey Publications All Rights Reserved.

The Fauré Élégie Study Book for Cello

Switching Between Extended and Closed Third Position
Measure 32a

Six Notes in a Bow
Measure 32a

©2017 C. Harvey Publications All Rights Reserved.

Learning the Notes
Measure 32b

Two Notes in a Bow
Measure 32b

Three Notes in a Bow
Measure 32b

The Fauré Élégie Study Book for Cello

Four Notes in a Bow
Measure 32b

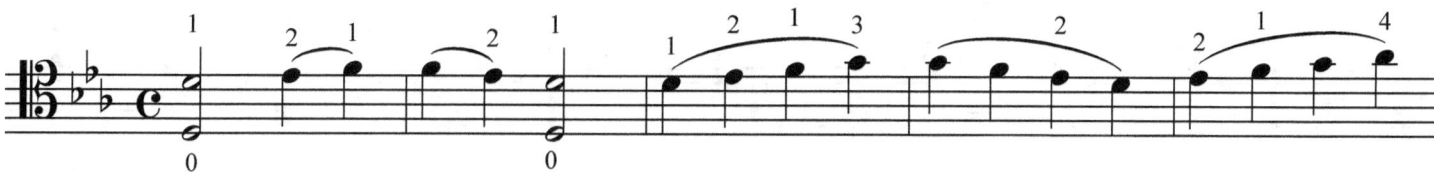

Rhythmic Shifting
Measure 32b

Working Towards Six Notes in a Bow
Measure 32b

©2017 C. Harvey Publications All Rights Reserved.

The Fauré Élégie Study Book for Cello
21

Learning the Notes
Measure 33a

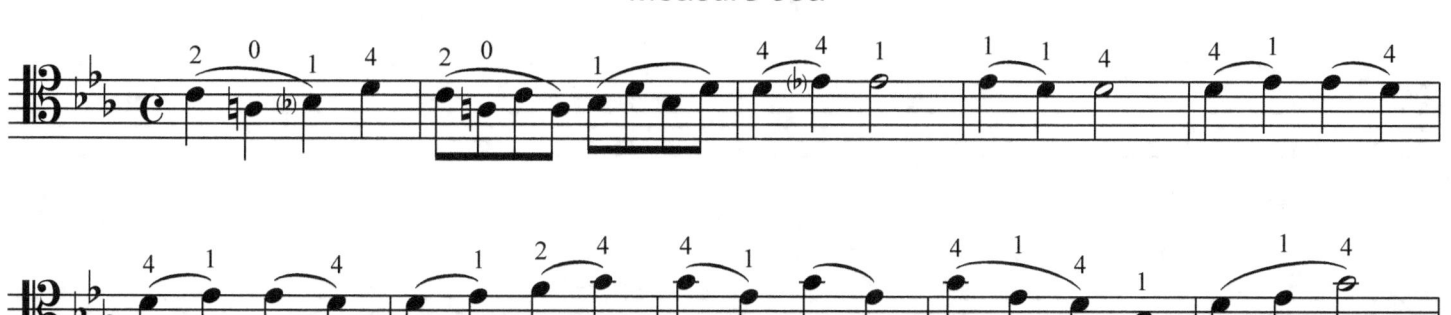

Learning More Notes
Measure 33a

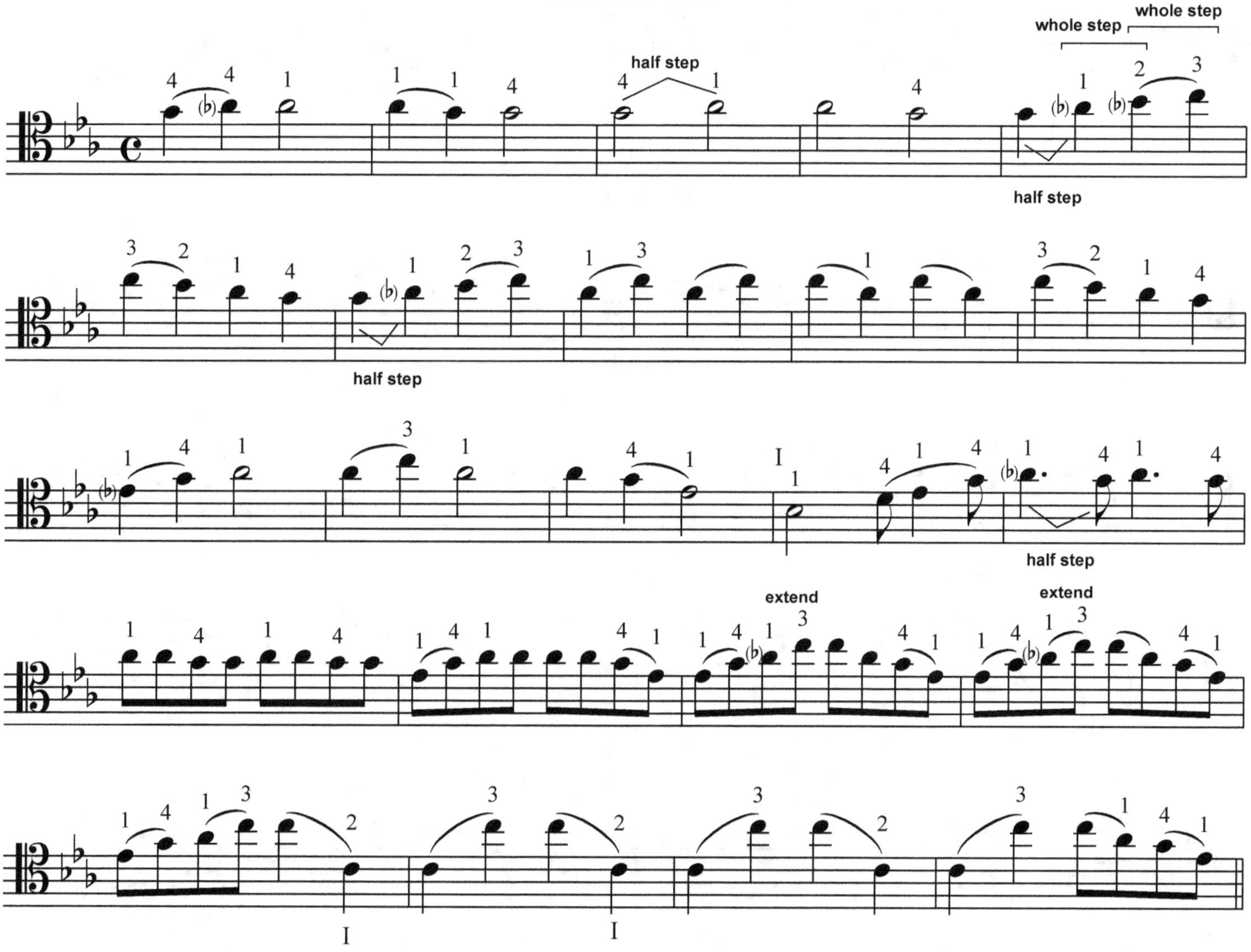

©2017 C. Harvey Publications All Rights Reserved.

Shifting Practice
Measure 33a

Finger Patterns
Measure 33a

Fluency
Measure 33a

The Fauré Élégie Study Book for Cello   23

The next five exercises are more advanced studies for measure 33a.

Agility
Measure 33a

Double Stops I
Measure 33a

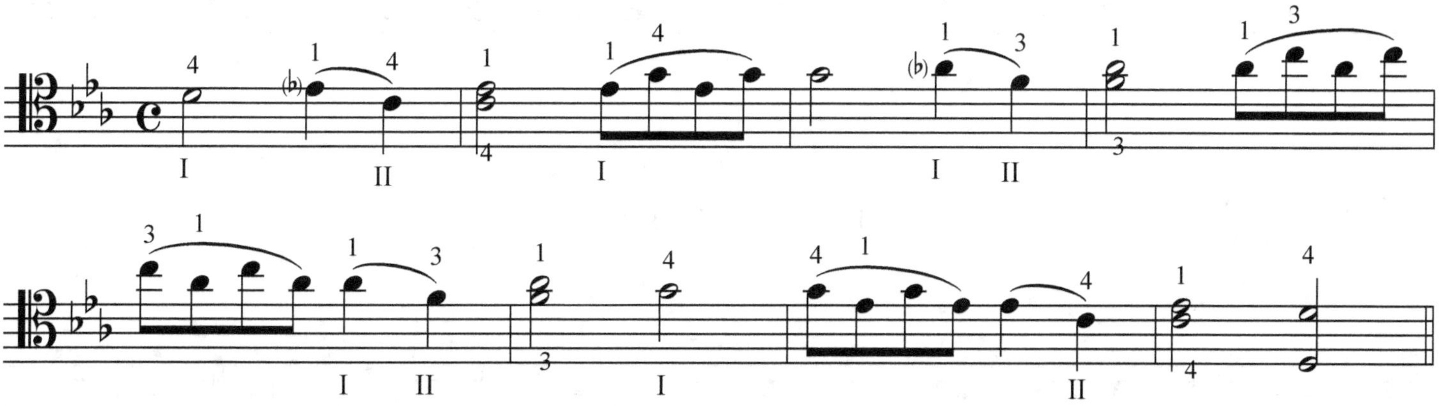

Double Stops II
Measure 33a

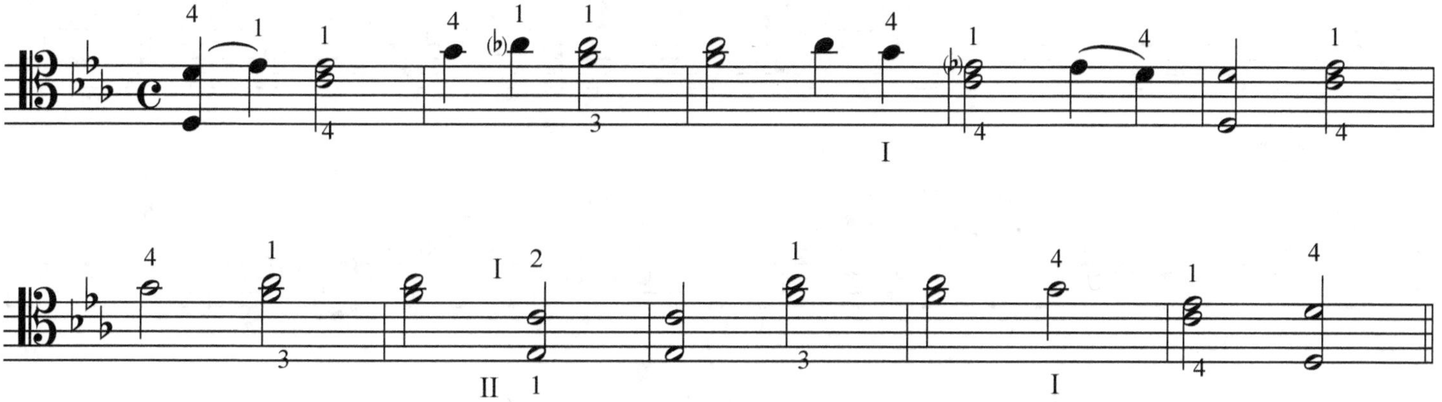

©2017 C. Harvey Publications All Rights Reserved.

Accuracy in Positions
Measure 33a

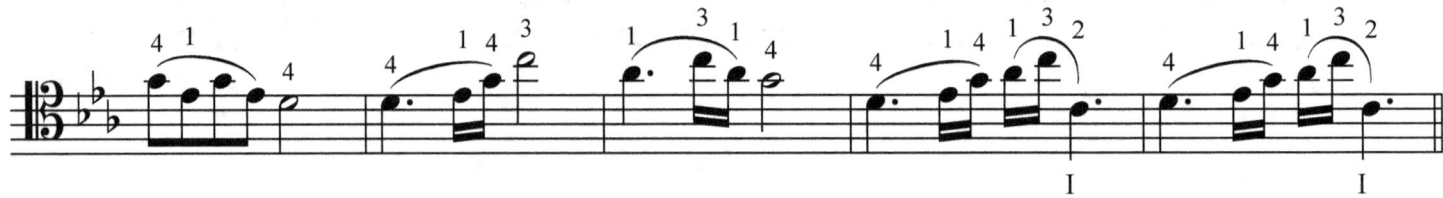

A Tricky Study for Fluency
Measure 33a

Learning the Notes
Measures 33b-34a

(Regular-level exercises begin again here.)

The Fauré Élégie Study Book for Cello

Agility: Measures 33b-34a

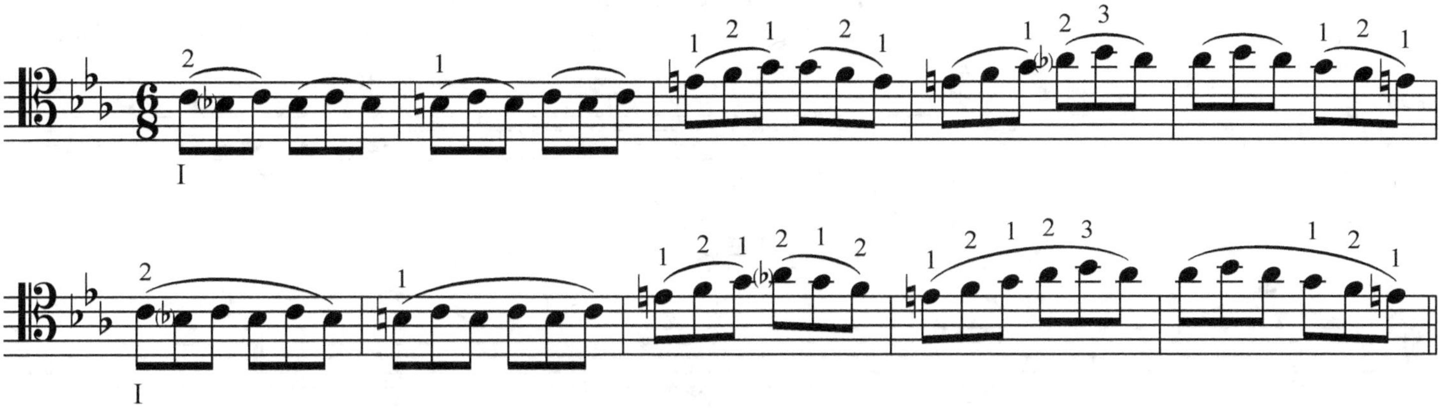

Working on Counting: Measure 33

Learning the Large Shift Across Strings: Measure 34a

©2017 C. Harvey Publications All Rights Reserved.

The Fauré Élégie Study Book for Cello

Learning the Notes
Measure 34b

Fluency
Measures 33B-34

Return to play the excerpt on p.13 before continuing with p.28.

©2017 C. Harvey Publications All Rights Reserved.

Élégie
Part Five: Measures 35-36a

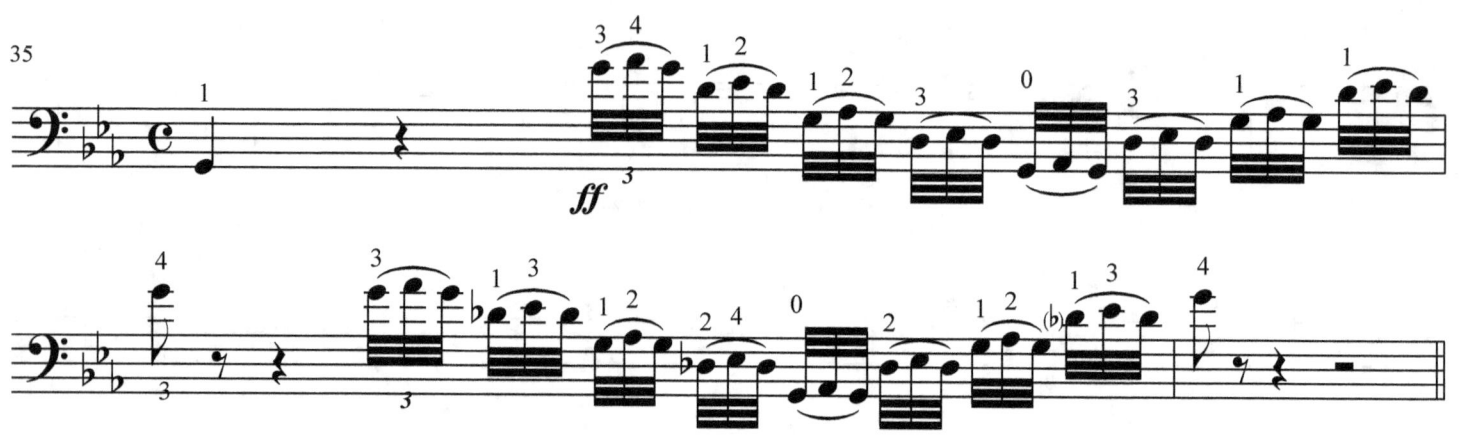

Exercises on pages 28-41 can be first played slowly, then faster, and eventually played as fast as possible.

Shifting to the Starting Note
Measure 35a

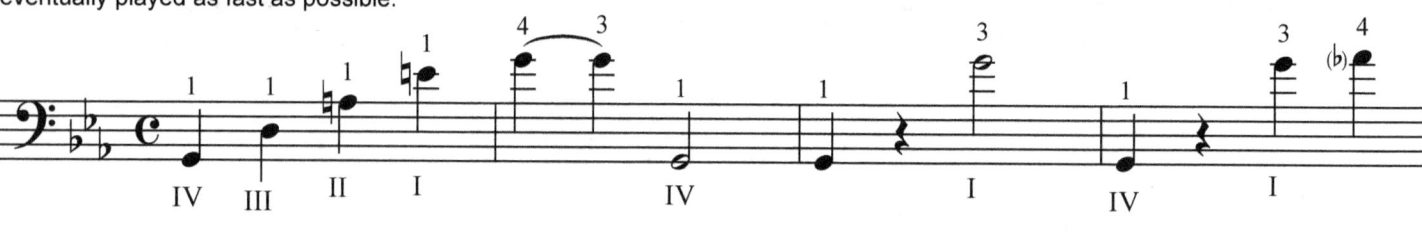

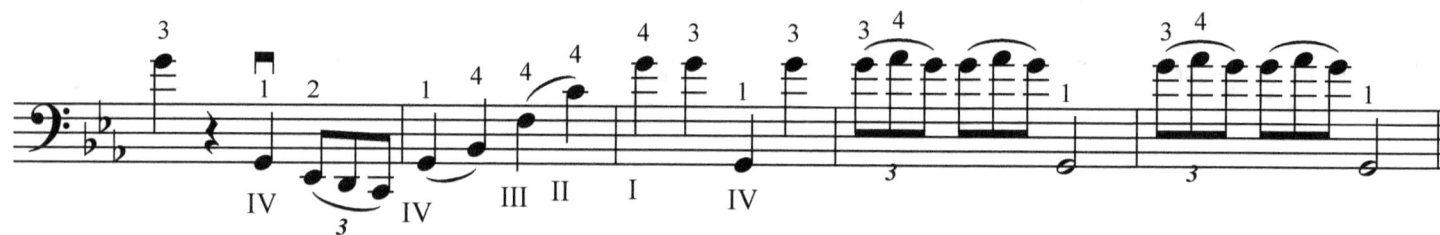

Learning the Backwards Shift
Measure 35

©2017 C. Harvey Publications All Rights Reserved.

Learning the Positions: Measure 35

Filling in the Other Notes in the Pattern: Measure 35

Shifting to the Right Place: Measure 35

Triplets I: Measure 35

All exercises: first Moderato, then Presto

Triplets II: Measure 35

Triplets III: Measure 35

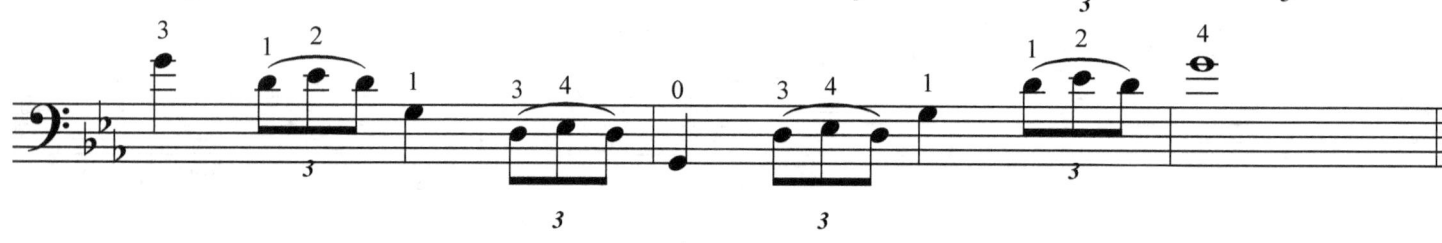

Triplets IV: Measure 35

The Fauré Élégie Study Book for Cello

Learning the Backwards Shift
Measure 35b

Learning the Positions
Measure 35b

Filling in the Other Notes in the Pattern
Measure 35b

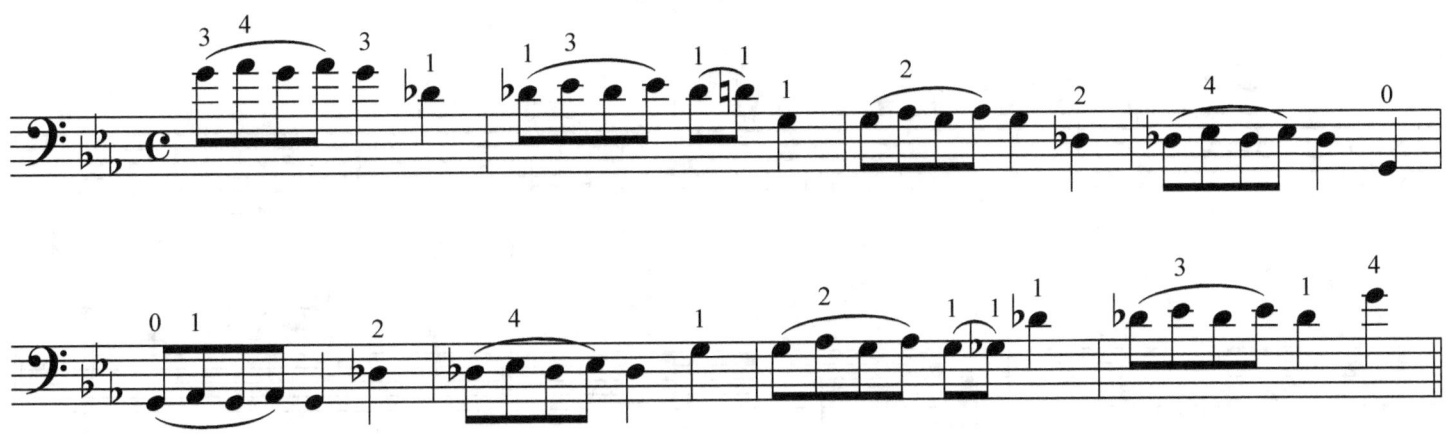

©2017 C. Harvey Publications All Rights Reserved.

Shifting to the Right Place: Measure 35b

Shifting Across Strings: Measure 35b

This exercise: first Moderato, then Presto

Triplets I: Measure 35b

The Fauré Élégie Study Book for Cello
All exercises: first Moderato, then Presto

Triplets II: Measure 35b

Triplets III: Measure 35b

Triplets IV: Measure 35b

All exercises: first Moderato, then Presto

Quick Shifting: Measure 35

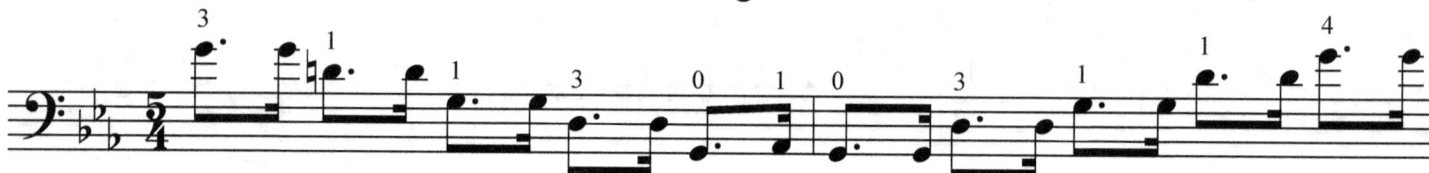

Fluency: Measure 35

Play the Patterns in One Position for Speed: Measure 35

Agility I
Measure 35

This exercise: first Moderato, then Presto

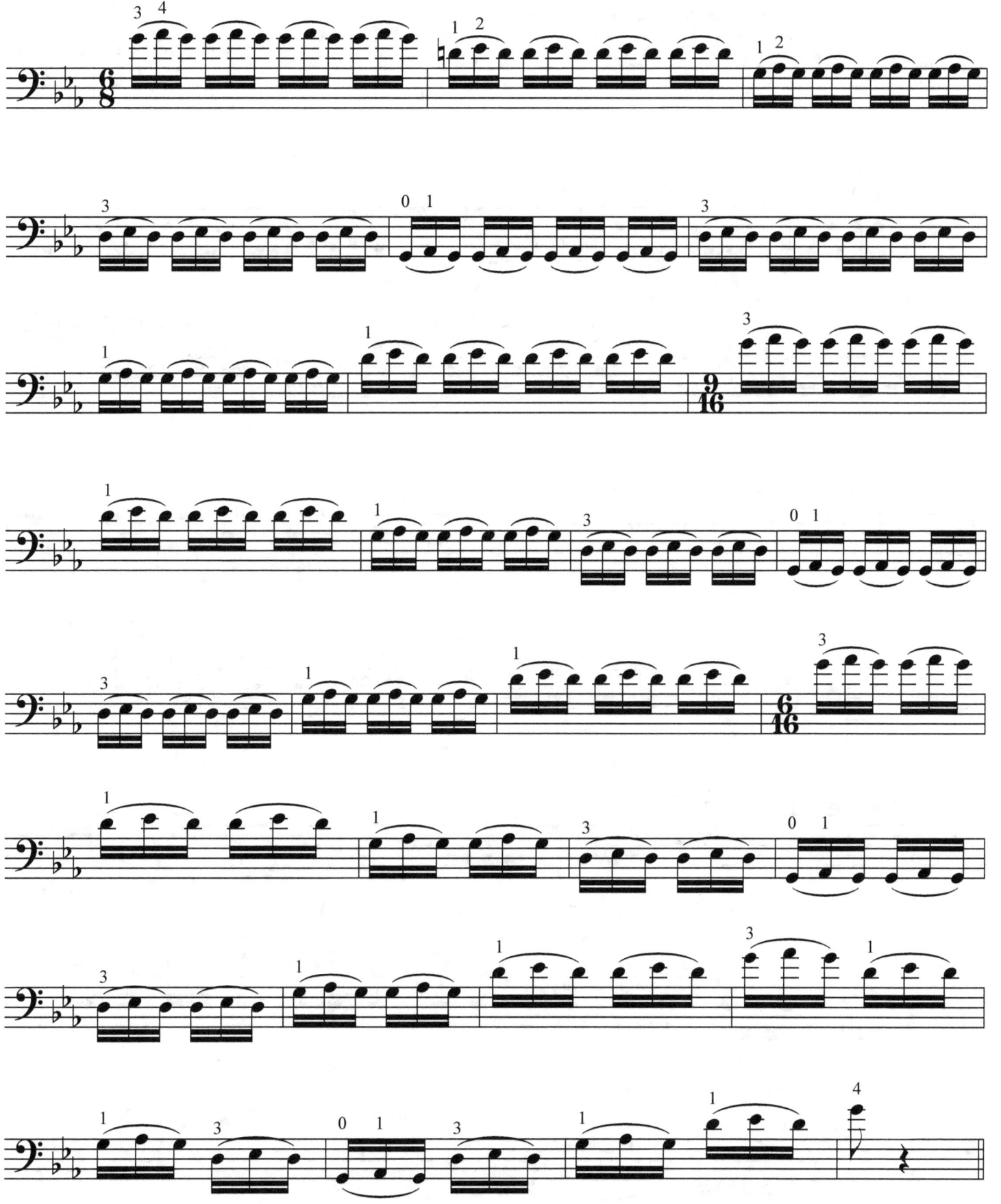

Agility II
Measure 35b

This exercise: first Moderato, then Presto

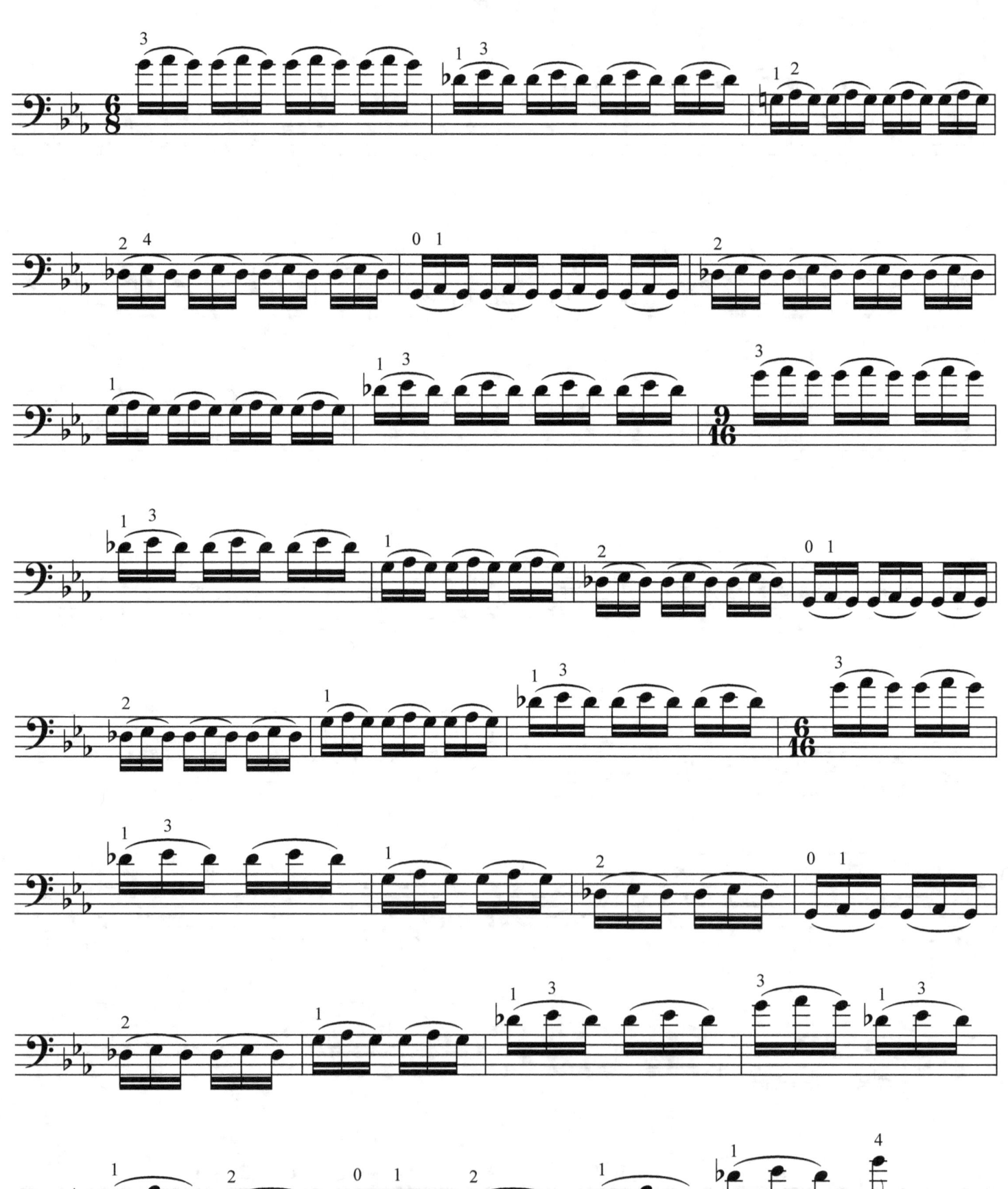

The Fauré Élégie Study Book for Cello

All exercises: first Moderato, then Presto

Finger Rhythms: Measures 35-36

Agility III: Measures 35-36

©2017 C. Harvey Publications All Rights Reserved.

Agility IV
Measures 35-36

All exercises: first Moderato, then Presto

Finger Rhythms for Speed
Measures 35-36

Agility V: Measures 35-36

The Fauré Élégie Study Book for Cello

All exercises: first Moderato, then Presto

The Fauré Élégie Study Book for Cello   41

This exercise: first Moderato, then Presto

Agility VIII: Measures 35-36

Double Stops for Intonation: Measures 35-36

Double Stops for Agility: Measures 35-36

Trills for Agility: Measures 35-36

Return to play the excerpt on p.28 before continuing with p.43.

Élégie
Part Six: Measure 37

Learning the Shifts
Measure 37

Faster Shifting
Measure 37

©2017 C. Harvey Publications All Rights Reserved.

The Fauré Élégie Study Book for Cello

All exercises: first Moderato, then Presto

Agility: Measure 37a

Fluency: Measure 37a

Rhythms: Measure 37a

Study for Speed: Measure 37a

©2017 C. Harvey Publications All Rights Reserved.

The Fauré Élégie Study Book for Cello
All exercises: first Moderato, then Presto

Agility: Measure 37b

Fluency: Measure 37b

Rhythms: Measure 37b

Study for Speed: Measure 37b

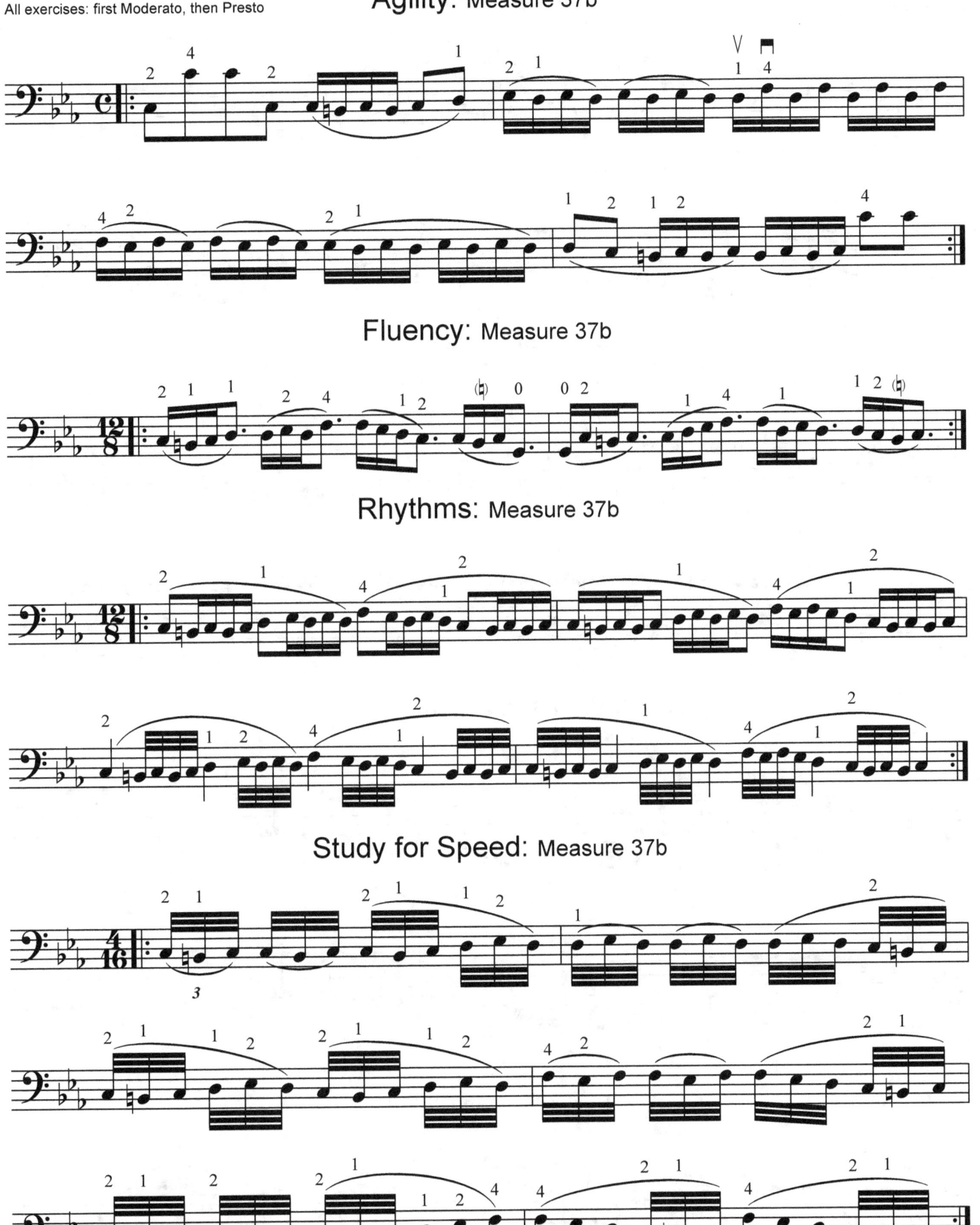

©2017 C. Harvey Publications All Rights Reserved.

All exercises: first Moderato, then Presto

Agility: Measure 37

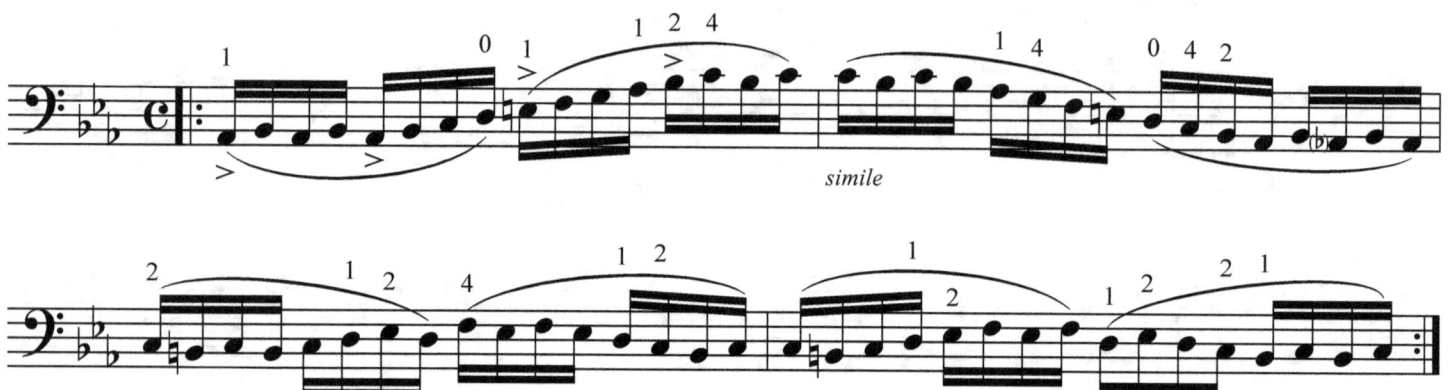

Staccato: Measure 37

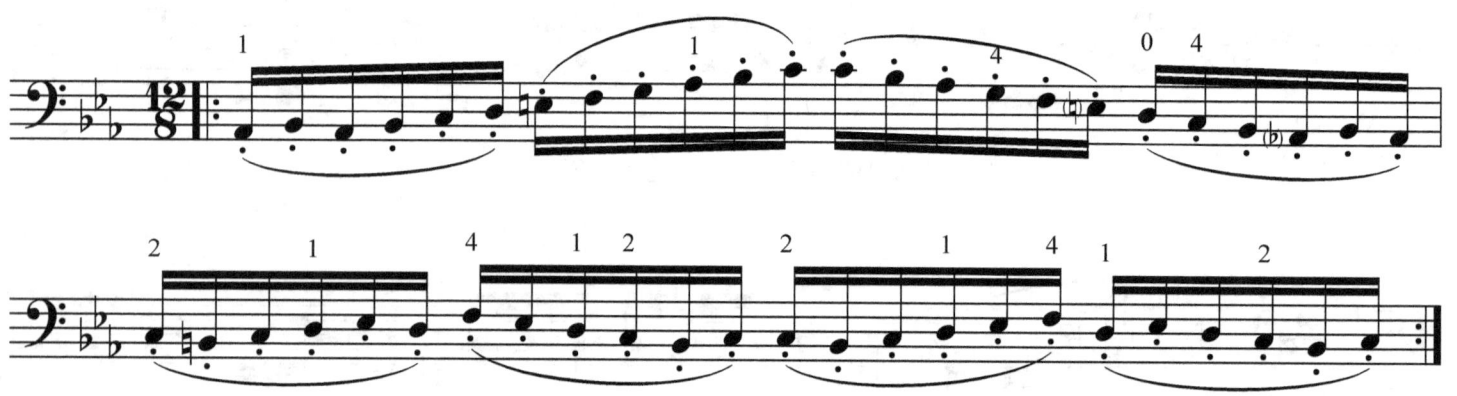

Rhythms: Measure 37

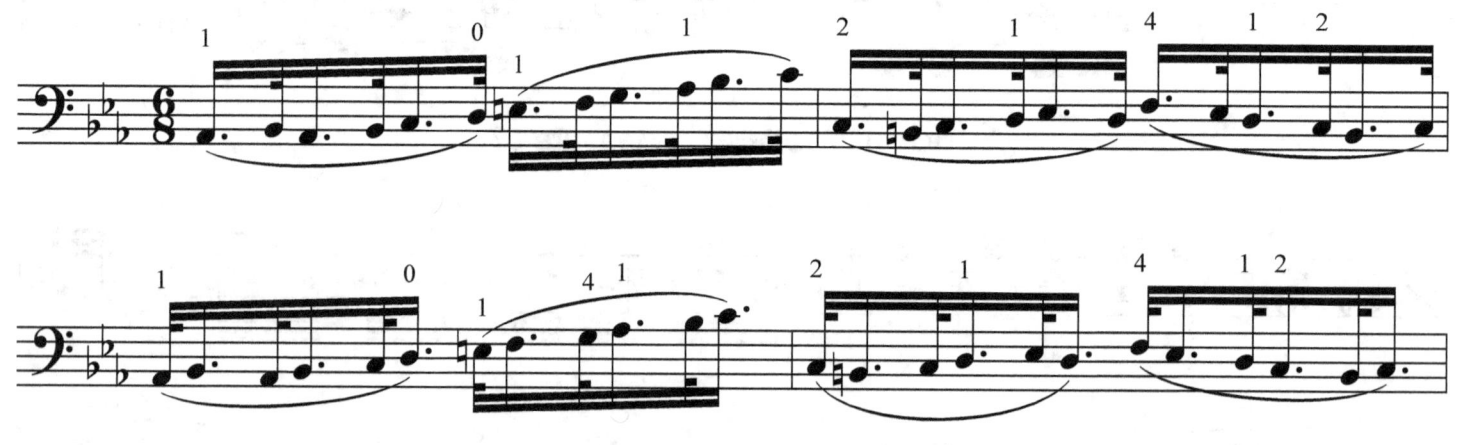

Fluency: Measure 37

Return to play the excerpt on p.43 before continuing with p.47.

Élégie
Part Seven: Measure 38

Learning the Shifts
Measure 38

48

All exercises: first Moderato, then Presto

The Fauré Élégie Study Book for Cello

Scale Spaces
Measure 38

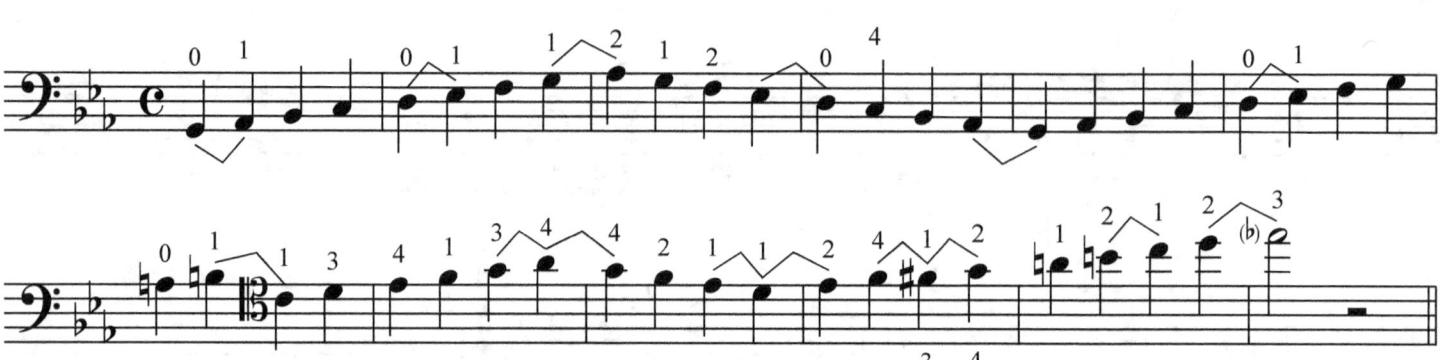

Transitioning to Faster Notes
Measure 38

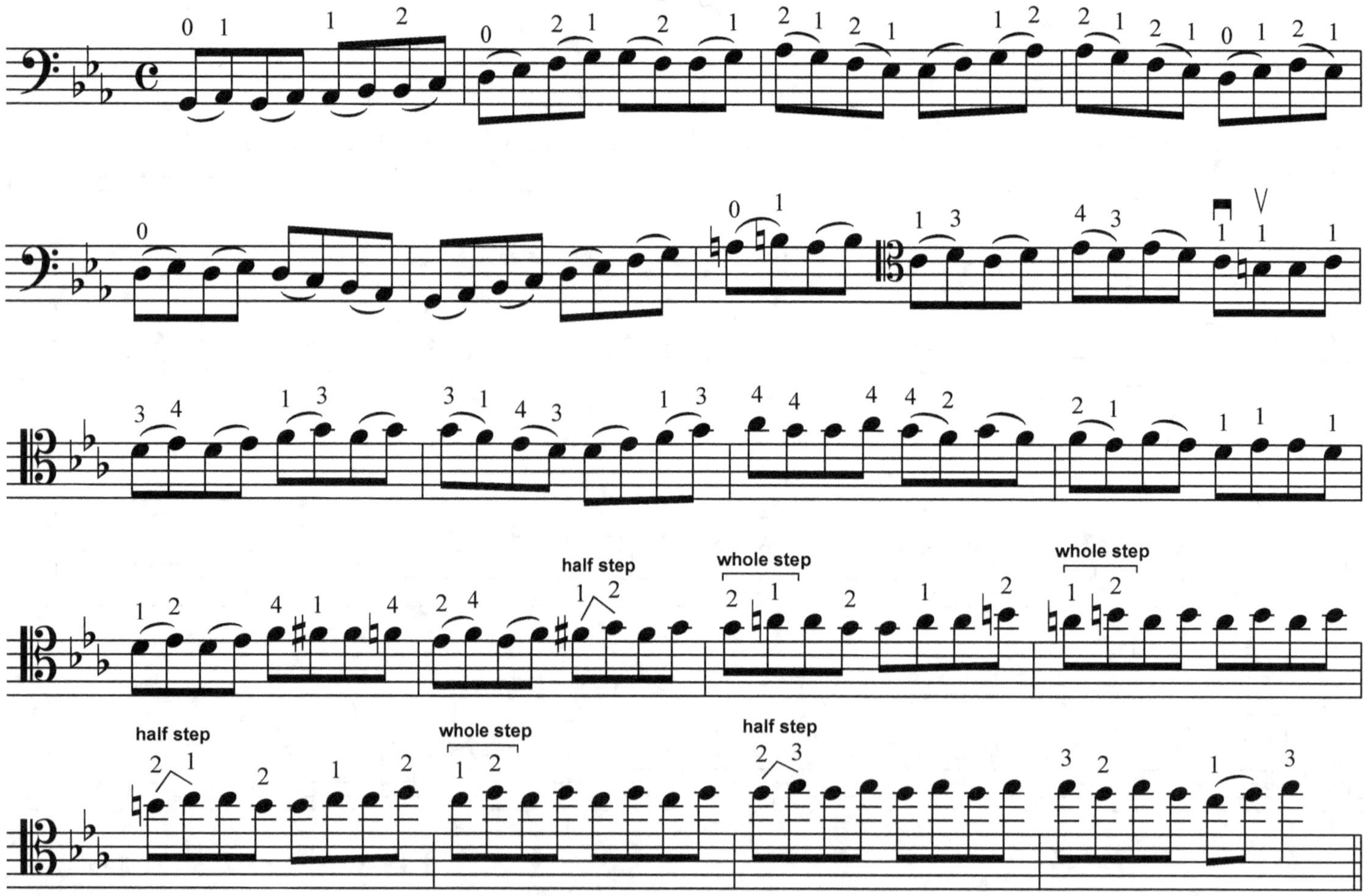

Longer Slurs
Measure 38

©2017 C. Harvey Publications All Rights Reserved.

The Fauré Élégie Study Book for Cello 49

Triplets
Measure 38

This exercise: first Moderato, then Presto

Working on the Highest Notes
Measure 38

Sixteenth Notes for Increased Speed
Measure 38

This exercise: first Moderato, then Presto

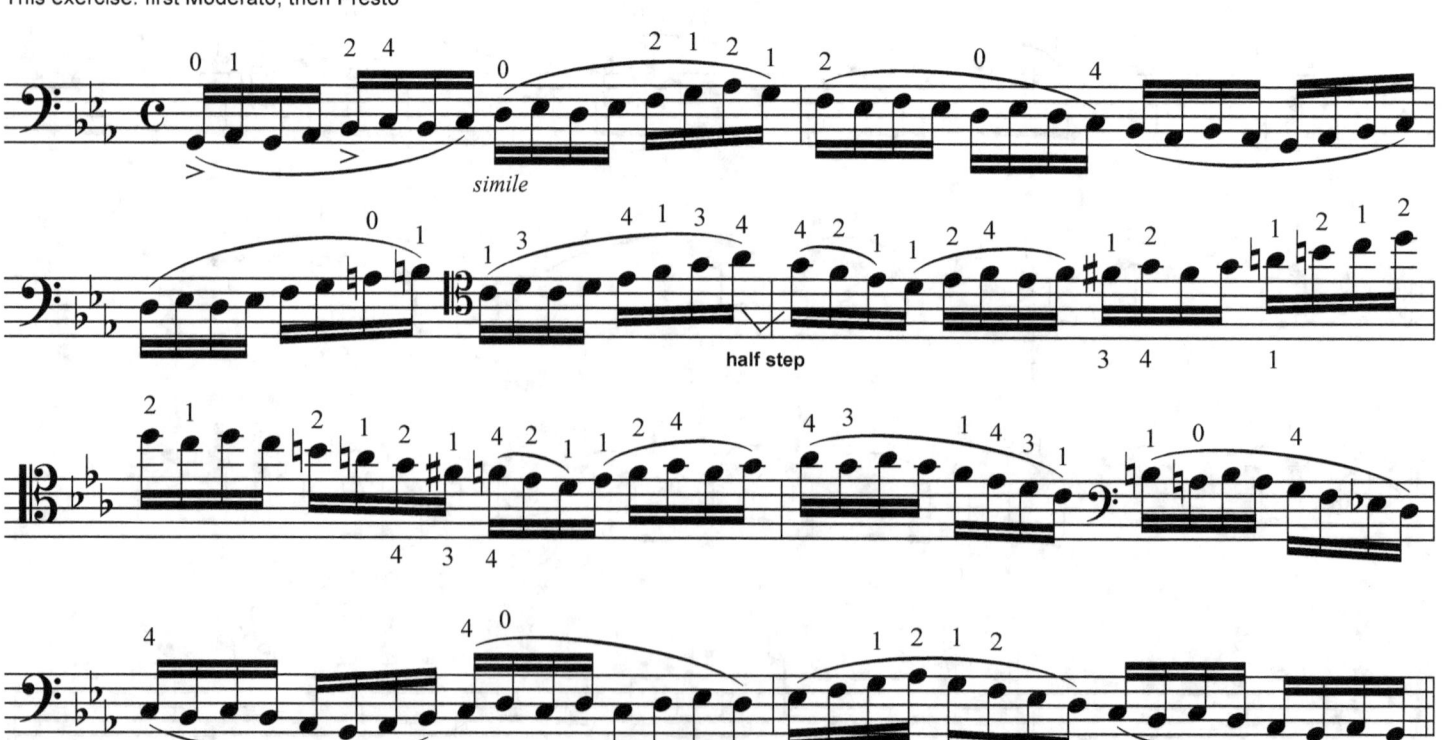

With these exercises, start at a slow tempo. Repeat a number of times, increasing the tempo each time.

Agility V: Measure 38

(vibrato)

Agility VI: Measure 38

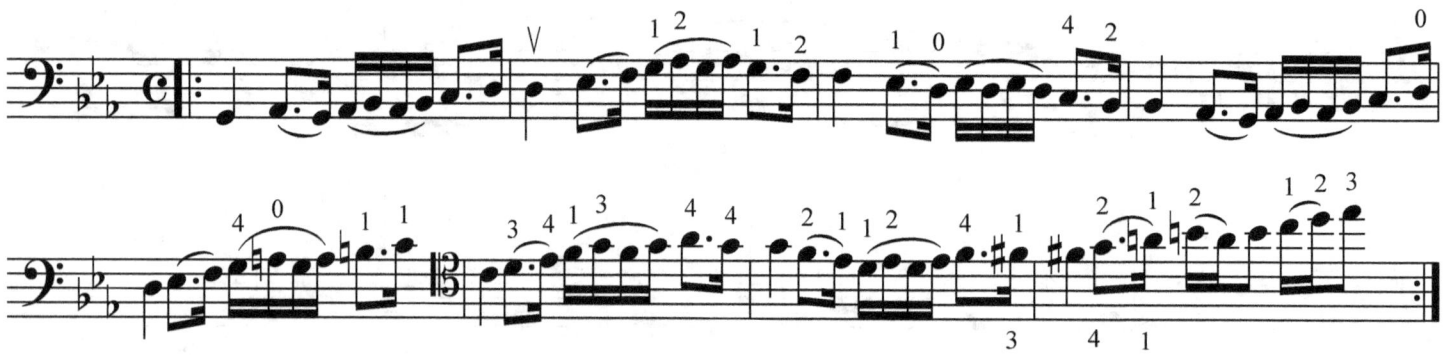

Agility VII: Measure 38

Agility VIII: Measure 38

©2017 C. Harvey Publications All Rights Reserved.

The Fauré Élégie Study Book for Cello

With these exercises, start at a slow tempo. Repeat a number of times, increasing the tempo each time.

Fluency I: Measure 38

Fluency II: Measure 38

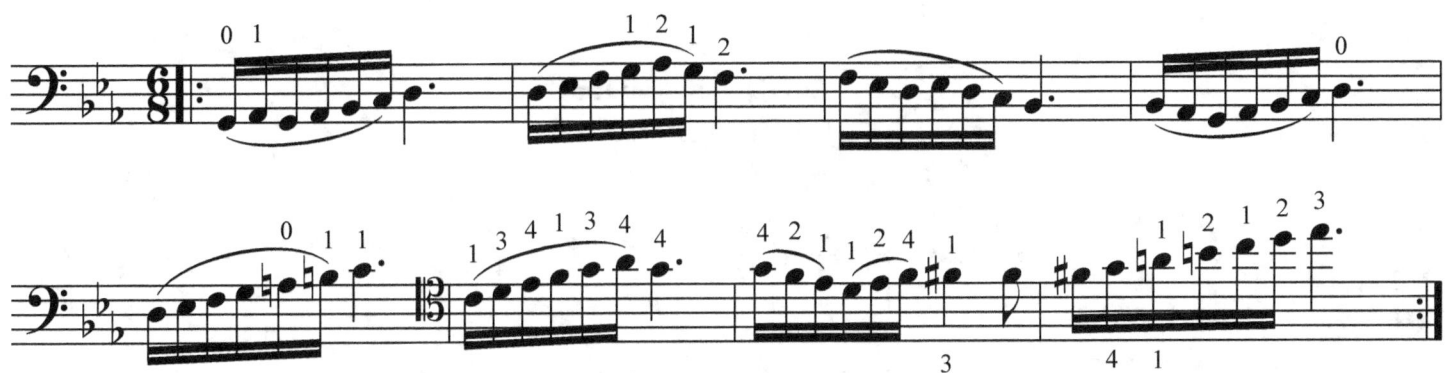

Articulation: Measure 38

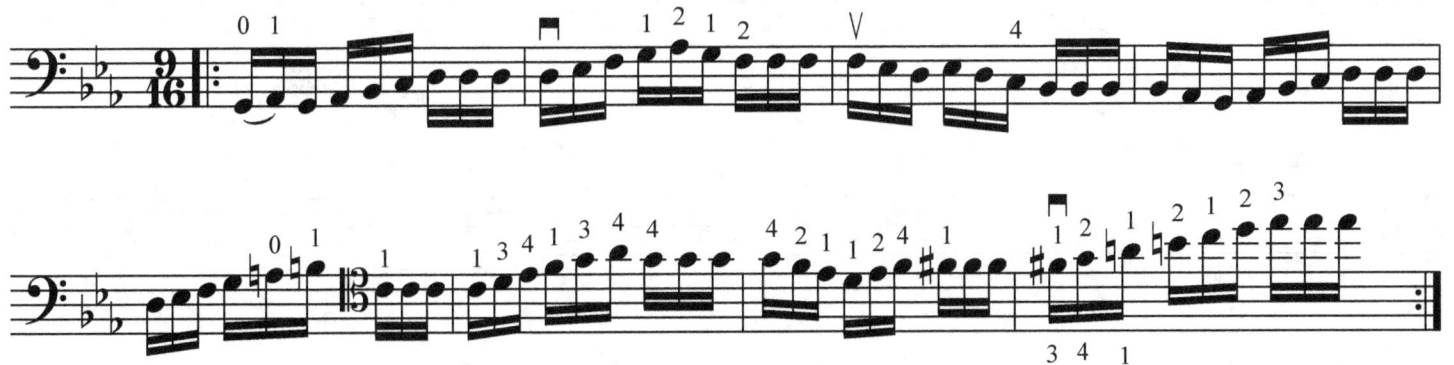

Fluency III: Measure 38

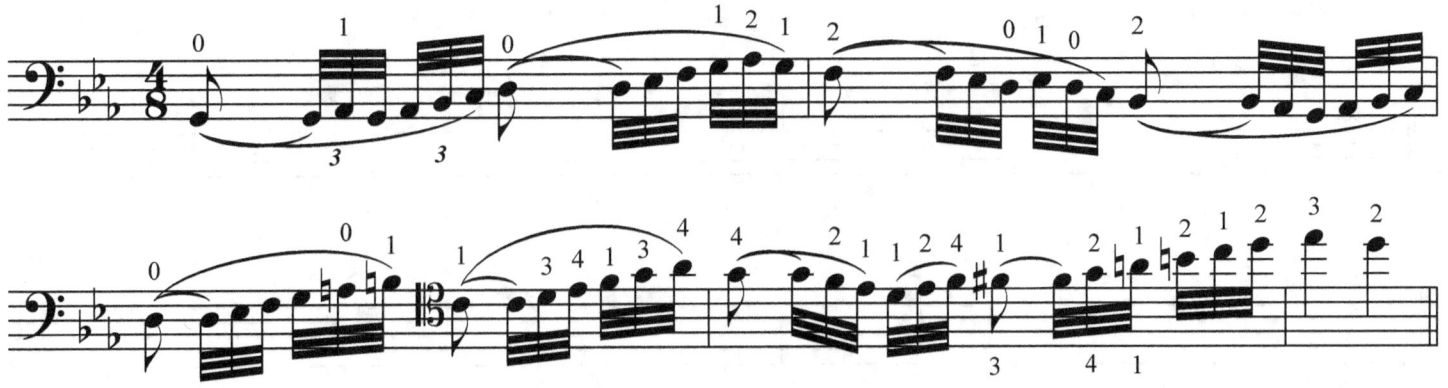

Return to play the excerpt on p.47 before continuing with p.54.

©2017 C. Harvey Publications All Rights Reserved.

Élégie

Part Eight: Measures 39-46

♪ = 66 **Tempo I**

Learning the Notes

Measures 39-40

Moderato

♩ = 80

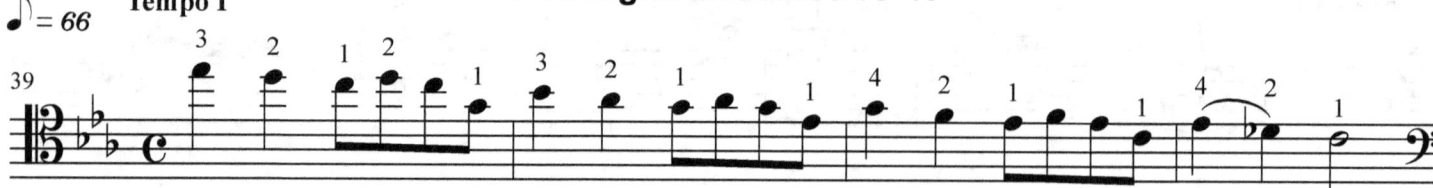

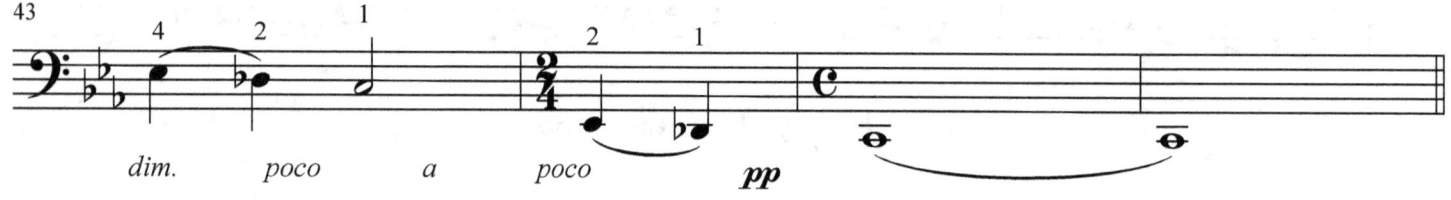

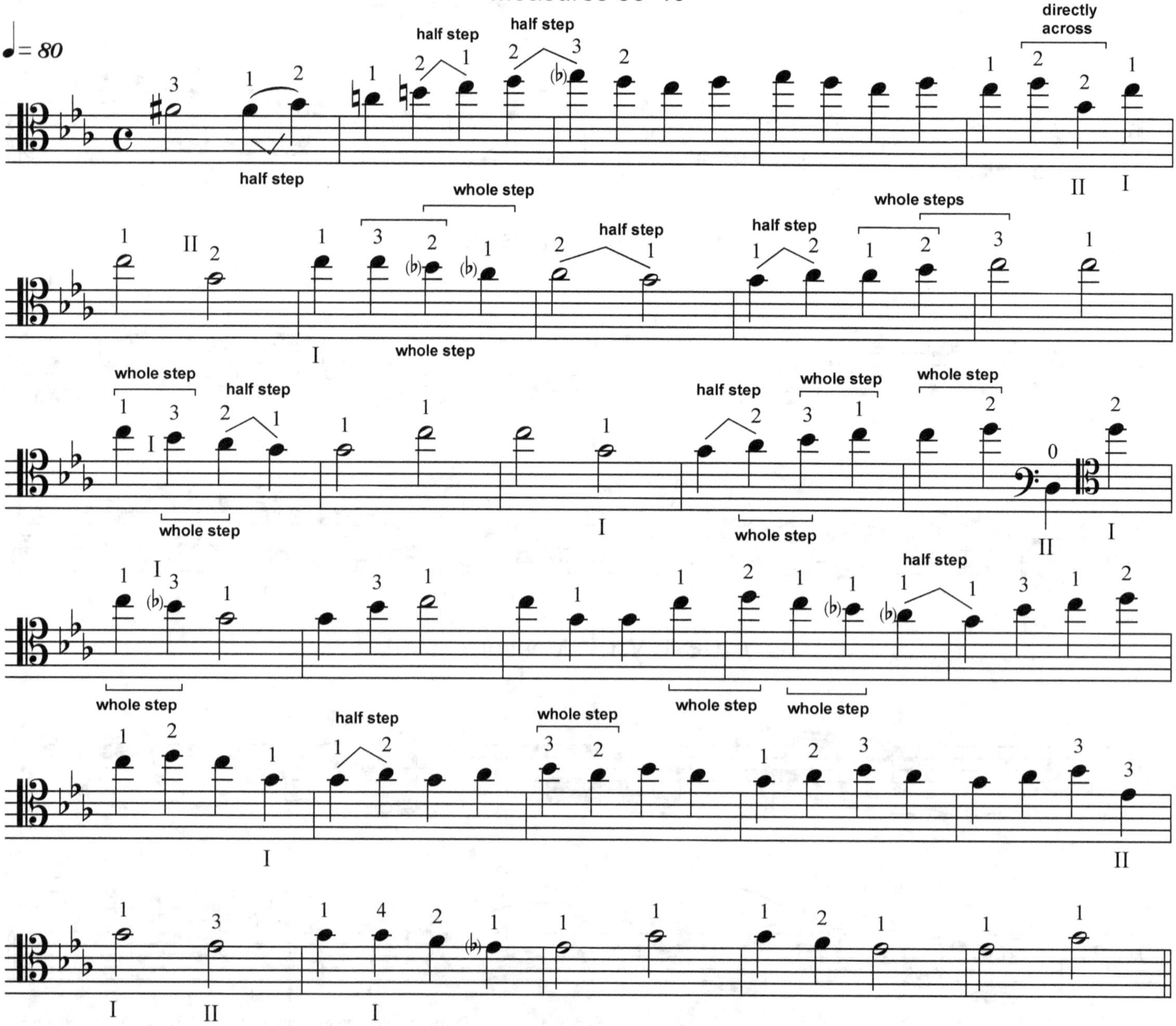

The Fauré Élégie Study Book for Cello

Learning the Notes
Measures 40-43

Shifting I
Measures 39-46

©2017 C. Harvey Publications All Rights Reserved.

Shifting II
Measures 39-46

Shifting III
Measures 39-46

Return to play the excerpt on p.54 before continuing with p.57.

Élégie
Part Nine: Measure 47-53 (end)

Learning the Notes
Measures 47-48

The Fauré Élégie Study Book for Cello

Shifting Practice
Measures 47-53

Expressive Shifting Study
Measures 47-53

Rhythm
Measures 47-53

Return to play the excerpt on p.57 before continuing with p.62.

This page left blank to eliminate page turns.

Élégie

Gabriel Fauré

The Fauré Élégie Study Book for Cello

Also available from www.charveypublications.com: CHP349
The Saint-Saens Cello Concerto No. 1 Study Book, Vol. 1

Concerto
Section One: Measures 1-7

Concerto, by Camille Saint-Saëns
Exercises by Cassia Harvey

Learning the Notes and the First Shift
Measures 1, 5

©2019 C. Harvey Publications All Rights Reserved.

www.ingramcontent.com/pod-product-compliance
Lightning Source LLC
Chambersburg PA
CBHW051423070526
44584CB00023B/3552